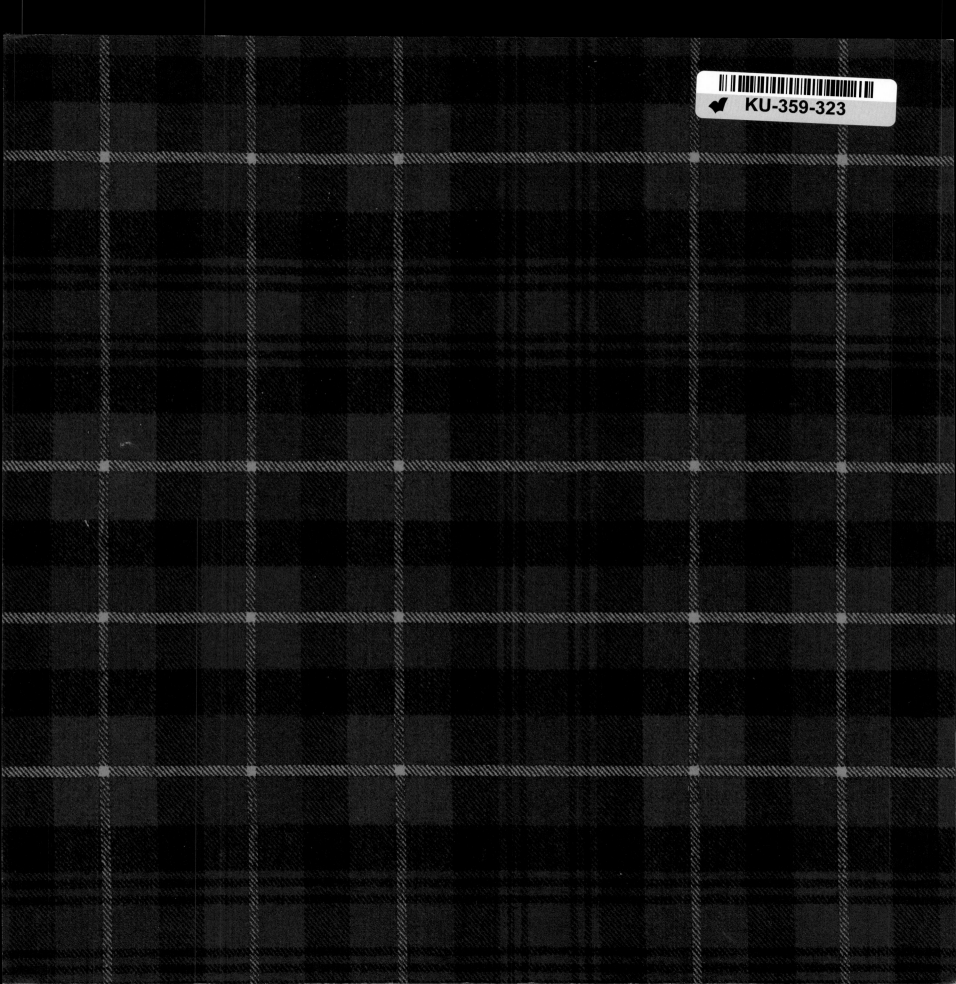

A picture of
FLEMINGS

CONTENTS

ROBERT FLEMING HOLDINGS LIMITED, 25 COPTHALL AVENUE, LONDON EC2R 7DR 01-638 5858

Text by Bill Smith of Flemings

Designed by The Astle Horman Partnership

Produced by Valin Pollen International PLC

Printed by The Oakley Press, Bristol

Set in Plantin by Text Filmsetters Limited

Dedication

This book is dedicated to the memory of David Donald.

Flemings is very proud of its collection of Scottish paintings which decorate its offices and give immense pleasure to visitors and staff alike. The success of the collection is entirely due to the inspiration and flair of David Donald who, during the seventeen years he was a director of the company, devoted so much wit and talent to assembling it. These pictures will, for many years to come, give the same pleasure to the people at Flemings and their friends as they once did to David himself. They are a splendid memorial to him.

J BURNETT-STUART

Robert Fleming Holdings Limited is the successor to a business which was started by Robert Fleming in Dundee in 1873 when he formed the first investment trust in Scotland. He moved to London in 1890 and became a leading figure in the investment trust industry in Scotland and England, which grew rapidly and played a prominent part in financing the growth of the North American economy.

The business he founded became a company in 1932, a year before he died, and it was by then one of the leading investment firms in the City of London. Since the Second World War the growth and diversification of the company has been continuous to the point where it is now a major international investment banking group.

The present group provides services which include investment management, banking, advice on corporate finance, mergers and acquisitions, as well as broking and dealing in securities. These services are offered to a wide range of customers including governments, companies large and small and, largely through Save and Prosper, to individuals. It also has a controlling interest in a Lloyd's insurance broker. The international scope of the group is very wide, with important operations in Japan, Hong Kong and Australia through Jardine Fleming (in partnership with Jardine Matheson), and in the USA through Eberstadt Fleming. It also has representation in France, Germany, Switzerland and the Middle East.

Although Flemings must be reckoned a substantial business, employing with its subsidiaries and associates worldwide almost 2,000 people, it is still a family firm with a friendly and informal atmosphere, something of which may be conveyed by this book about its collection of pictures.

Abbreviations

ARSA   Associate of the Royal Scottish Academy
RSA   Royal Scottish Academician
PRSA   President of the Royal Scottish Academy
HRSA   Honorary Member of the Royal Scottish Academy
RSW   Royal Scottish Society of Painters in Water-colours
PRSW   President of the Royal Scottish Society of Painters in Water-colours
HRSW   Honorary Member of the Royal Scottish Society of Painters in Water-colours
ARA   Associate of the Royal Academy of Arts
RA   Royal Academician
RHA   Royal Hibernian Academician
RWS   Member of the Royal Society of Painters in Water-Colours
RI   Royal Institute of Painters in Water Colours
RP   Member of the Royal Society of Portrait Painters

Figures in parentheses denote Flemings' collection number

The Nineteenth Century

The second half of the eighteenth century had witnessed a blossoming of the intellectual and cultural life of Scotland. David Hume, Adam Smith, Robert Burns, Sir Walter Scott and Henry Raeburn contributed much to this upsurge, as, to a lesser extent, did Allan Ramsay and Robert Adam, both of whom settled in London. However, although there were a number of notable Scottish painters at the beginning of the nineteenth century, it was not until well into that century that there emerged a Scottish school of painting in terms of an identifiable Scottish style. In general, Scottish painters in the first half of the century were influenced by art in Rome or London rather than by a native style. All too often, they felt that to be successful they had to move to London, which was the principal source of patronage.

Three major figures dominated Scottish painting in the opening decades of the nineteenth century: Henry Raeburn (1756-1823) in portraiture, Alexander Nasmyth (1758-1840) in landscape and David Wilkie (1785-1841) in genre. Born in Edinburgh, the second son of a textile mill owner, Raeburn painted portrait miniatures while apprenticed to the Edinburgh goldsmith James Gilliland. Largely self-taught, he spent two months in the London studio of Sir Joshua Reynolds in 1784 before going on to study in Rome. On his return in 1786 he soon established himself as the leading portrait painter in Edinburgh. But he was not without his early critics (including Sir Walter Scott), who accused him of bluntness in his portrayals, lack of finish and weakness in anatomical drawing. He was knighted in 1822 and was appointed the King's Limner for Scotland in the following year. Nasmyth, whom Wilkie called 'the father of Scottish landscape', was also born in Edinburgh and studied at the Trustees' Academy and in the studio of Allan Ramsay in London. On his return to Edinburgh after spending two years in Italy, he took up portrait painting before concentrating on landscape. David Wilkie (qv) was an outstanding exponent of domestic and, later, historical genre, with an exceptional gift for observation of character. He moved to London when he was 20 and became an immediate success. When his 'Chelsea Pensioners' was exhibited at the Royal Academy in 1822, the pressure to see the picture was so great that a crush barrier – an unheard of expedient – had to be erected in front of the picture to prevent its damage.

Of the painters born in the first two or three decades of the 19th century, only William Dyce (1806-1864) and David Scott (1806-1849) even approached the stature of Raeburn or Wilkie. Both were figure painters. Born in Aberdeen, Dyce studied at the Trustees' Academy in Edinburgh and the Royal Academy Schools in London and made several visits to Rome. A polymath, he eventually became Director of the London School of Design. David Scott was born in Edinburgh and trained as an engraver in the family firm before taking up painting. He was a painter of great vision, whose work was admired by fellow artists but not by the general public. He was made an Academician of the Scottish Academy when only 24.

Other noteworthy painters during the period include: in portraiture, Francis Grant (1803-1878) and Daniel Macnee (1806-1882), who became Presidents of the Royal Academy and the Royal Scottish Academy respectively; in landscape, Horatio McCulloch (1805-1867) (qv); in figure painting, Robert Scott Lauder (1803-1869), who became the last and most influential of the Directors of the Trustees' Academy, George Harvey (1806-1876), Thomas Duncan (1807-1845), John Phillip (1817-1867), Joseph Noel Paton (1821-1901) and William Fettes Douglas (1822-1891) – both Harvey and Fettes Douglas became Presidents of the Royal Scottish Academy.

Apart from the short-lived Foulis Academy (1753-75) in Glasgow, Scotland did not have a training school for artists until 1760, when the Trustees' Academy was established in Edinburgh by the Board of Trustees for Manufactures, a body set up in 1727 by the Government at Westminster. It was the first 'Drawing Academy' maintained at public expense, but it was not a true art school until John Graham was appointed Master in 1798. The Trustees' Academy at first taught drawing from casts, but later it introduced drawing from life and classes in design and colour. In 1852, following complaints by the President of the Royal Scottish Academy that the standard of work was poor, Robert Scott Lauder, who had himself been a student in 1822-3 and had deputised as Master in 1829-30, was appointed Director of the drawing, life and colour classes. Scott Lauder's inspiring personality and teaching were powerful influences on his students. William Hardie in 'Scottish Painting 1837-1939' writes that Scott Lauder's 'nine years in charge of the Trustees' Academy clearly mark a watershed in Scottish painting'. His students included William Quiller Orchardson (1832-1910), the figurative painter, Peter Graham (1836-1921) and John MacWhirter (1839-1911), both landscape painters, Hugh Cameron (1835-1918), the genre painter, William McTaggart (1835-1910) (qv), the landscape painter and the most outstanding and original of Scott Lauder's pupils, George Paul Chambers (1833-1878), the figurative and landscape painter, the brothers John Burr (1831-1893) and Alexander Burr (1835-1899), both genre painters, Thomas Graham (1840-1906), the genre, historical and portrait painter, and John Pettie (1839-1893), the figurative and historical painter. Although only Cameron, Chambers and McTaggart remained in Scotland, Scott Lauder's pupils may be described as constituting the first genuine school of Scottish painters.

Scottish painting in the nineteenth century was fostered by the establishment of a number of bodies, the principal object of which was to bring art before a much wider audience than hitherto and thus help Scottish artists. The Institution for the Encouragement of the Fine Arts in Scotland was founded in 1819 and received its Royal Charter in 1827. The Institution held loan exhibitions of Old Masters and, later, of paintings by contemporary artists. However, it was run by 'noblemen and gentlemen' – artists were excluded from having any hand in its affairs – and this led to disillusionment and discontent on the part of the artists. Consequently, in 1826 a group of painters founded the Scottish Academy, which was to be run by and for artists. It was modelled on the Royal Academy in London and was to hold annual exhibitions of the work of members and invited artists, the pictures being for sale. In the first few years of the Academy's existence there was intense rivalry between the two bodies, but the Academy's exhibitions gained in popularity, whereas those of the Royal Institution declined. The Academy's exhibition in 1829 was so successful that the Royal Institution capitulated and decided not to mount any further exhibitions. Instead, the latter concentrated on acquiring pictures and prints for its collection, which, together with the Academy's pictures and private endowments, was to form the basis of the Scottish national collection. Although the squabbling between the two bodies continued, the Academy prospered and was an important influence on Scottish painting. It gained its Royal Charter in 1838. A Life School was started in 1859. But soon it was overtaken by another problem, on this occasion largely of its own making. The early membership of the Academy had comprised the best painters in Scotland, but in the second half of the century it was accused of making it difficult, if not impossible, for artists not living in Edinburgh to become members. This attitude caused ill-feeling and resentment on the part of artists living in other cities, particularly in Glasgow. It was not until the last decade of the century that, despite some continued opposition, artists not living

in Edinburgh were admitted as Associates. In the meantime, the Academy's monopoly of large exhibitions ended with the founding of the Glasgow Institute of the Fine Arts in 1861 and the Glasgow Art Club in 1867. These bodies provided an outlet for the exhibition (and sale) of pictures by Glasgow artists, who were denied access to the Academy.

Scottish painting in the final decades of the century was characterised by a movement towards Realism and away from sentimental anecdote and the academic precepts of the artistic Establishment in Edinburgh. Nowhere was this movement stronger than in Glasgow, where an important new school of painting was being born.

Artists represented

ROBERT WEIR ALLAN, RWS, RSW

1851-1942

Born in Glasgow, Allan trained there and in Paris under Julian and Cabanel. Arthur Melville (qv) was a considerable influence. Allan's subjects are mainly landscapes of the North East Coast of Scotland, fishing villages, harbours and fishing boats, painted en plein air. He travelled extensively in Europe, toured India in 1891-2, went to Japan in 1907, and visited North Africa in 1911-12. Allan settled in London in 1881.

SAMUEL BOUGH, RSA

1822-1878

Born in Carlisle, Bough worked in the Town Clerk's Office in Carlisle for two years before deciding to take up painting full-time. At first he travelled around the North of England with a band of gypsies, sketching them and the landscape, before working as a scene-painter in Manchester and Glasgow. It was in Glasgow in 1848 that, encouraged by Sir Daniel Macnee, he decided to concentrate on landscape painting, for which he became noted. His art was dominated by his early training (he was largely self-taught) and his work for the theatre. His watercolours are particularly fine. Bough settled in Edinburgh in 1855 and was elected ARSA in 1856 and RSA in 1875.

ROBERT McGOWN COVENTRY, ARSA, RSW

1855-1914

Born in Glasgow, Coventry studied at Glasgow School of Art and in Paris. His subjects are mainly landscapes and coastal scenes in Scotland and also in Belgium and Holland. The Hague School was a considerable influence on his work. In the 1890's he visited the Middle East. He was elected ARSA in 1906.

JAMES DOCHARTY, ARSA

1829-1878

Born in the Vale of Leven, Dunbartonshire, Docharty was a pattern designer for calico-printing and worked in Paris for a time. It was not until he was over 30 that he was able to take up landscape painting full-time. He was largely self-taught. Living in Glasgow, he painted subjects in the West of Scotland, the Trossachs and the Hebrides. In 1876, forced south by failing health, he travelled to Egypt by way of France and Italy. He died in 1878 shortly after his return, only a few months after he was elected ARSA.

THOMAS FAED, RA, ARSA

1826-1900

Born near Gatehouse of Fleet, Faed studied at the Trustees' Academy in Edinburgh. His elder brother, John (1820-1902), was also a painter and a younger brother, James, was a mezzotint engraver who reproduced some of the work of his two brothers. Thomas Faed continued the genre tradition of Wilkie, specialising in paintings of peasant life with a strong accent on pathos; it was said that he favoured 'departures for the colonies or heaven'! He first exhibited at the Royal Scottish Academy when he was 18 and was elected ARSA in 1849 when he was only 23. In 1852 he moved to London, where he became a close friend of Charles Dickens. He was elected ARA in 1861 and RA in 1864.

DAVID FARQUHARSON, ARA, ARSA, RSW

1840-1907

Born in Blairgowrie, Farquharson was originally a housepainter, but gave that up to concentrate on art. He moved to Edinburgh in 1872. Largely self-taught, he was influenced by the Hague School painters. He painted in Scotland, England and Holland; his subjects are mainly landscapes and coastal scenes. He moved to London in 1882 and later settled in Sennen Cove, Cornwall, although he often revisited Scotland. He was elected ARSA in 1882 and ARA in 1906.

JOSEPH FARQUHARSON, RA

1846-1935

Born in Edinburgh, where his father was a doctor and amateur artist, Farquharson trained at the Trustees' Academy and the life class of the Royal Scottish Academy. He exhibited at the RSA when he was only 15. He came of an old Aberdeenshire family and his lovely wooded estate of Finzean in the Dee Valley provided the settings for many of his landscapes. His reputation was based on his winter landscapes depicting either light reflected off snow or blizzard conditions. He was influenced by Peter Graham, an established Scottish landscape painter and a family friend, and was very friendly with John Singer Sargent. He spent three or four winters from 1880 in Paris at the studio of Carolus-Duran, exhibiting at the Salon in 1881. In 1885 he visited Egypt. Farquharson was elected ARA in 1900 and RA in 1915.

JOHN B FLEMING

1792-1845

Little is known of Fleming's life other than that he was born and lived in Greenock and painted landscapes, especially lochs. Like John Knox (qv), whose landscape technique he followed, Fleming was commissioned by Joseph Swan to engrave views for Swan's 'Views of Glasgow' (1828) and 'Views on the Clyde' (1830).

WILLIAM ALFRED GIBSON

1866-1931

Born in Glasgow, Gibson gave up a business career to concentrate on landscape painting. Largely self-taught, he was influenced by Corot and the painters of the Hague School. He worked mainly in Scotland, England, Holland and France.

EDWARD HARGITT, RI

1835-1895

Born in Edinburgh, Hargitt was a landscape painter, having been a pupil of Horatio McCulloch (qv). He was also well known as an ornithologist. He exhibited at the Royal Academy and elsewhere from 1853 to 1881, moving to London in 1867. He was elected an Associate of the Royal Institute of Painters in Water Colours in 1867 and a Member in 1871.

JOHN HENDERSON

1860-1924

Born in Glasgow, Henderson was the son of Joseph Henderson (1832-1908), who was the most prominent artist in that city of his generation. His younger brother, Joseph Morris Henderson (1863-1936), was also a painter and his sister became the second wife of William McTaggart (qv). John Henderson trained in his father's studio and then at Glasgow School of Art under Robert Greenlees. Typical subjects are coastal scenes and landscapes, often with children. His soft style, with light colours, is typical of the Scottish impressionist school and very reminiscent of the work of his near contemporary Robert Gemmell Hutchison (1855-1936). In common with many Glasgow artists of the period he also exhibited in Munich and at the Great Fair in Berlin in 1894, where he had considerable success.

ROBERT HOPE, RSA

1869-1936

Hope was born in Edinburgh and lived there all his life. He gave up a career as a lithographer and book illustrator to study at the RSA Schools. He specialised in portraits, genre and, later, landscape. He was elected ARSA in 1911 and RSA in 1925 and was President of the Society of Scottish Artists in 1910.

JOHN KNOX

1778-1845

Born in Paisley, where his father was a yarn merchant, Knox moved to Glasgow in 1799. He painted landscape and marine subjects, particularly in Glasgow, the

West of Scotland and the Clyde estuary, but also in the Lake District (his wife came from Cumberland) and Brussels. He was an exponent of the classical landscape style of Jacob More (1740?-1793) and Alexander Nasmyth with whom he is thought to have studied. In turn, Horatio McCulloch, Daniel Macnee and William Leighton Leitch (1804-1883) were pupils of Knox. He lived in London from 1828 to 1836 and moved to Keswick in 1840.

CHARLES LEES, RSA

1800-1880

Born in Cupar, Fife, Lees studied portraiture in Edinburgh as a pupil of Raeburn. He spent several years in Rome, returning to Edinburgh where he worked for the rest of his life. He was elected RSA in 1829, acting as Treasurer from 1868 until his death in 1880. Lees specialised in outdoor sporting scenes, particularly skating and, later, landscapes.

HORATIO McCULLOCH, RSA

1805-1867

Born in Glasgow, McCulloch was a house-painter in that city, painted snuff-boxes in Cumnock, and coloured anatomical plates for Lizars in Edinburgh, before deciding to concentrate on landscape painting. Along with Daniel Macnee and W L Leitch, he studied under John Knox in Glasgow. His early subjects were all near Glasgow, but later he worked mainly in the Highlands, frequently painting en plein air. He was influenced by the work of Rev. John Thomson of Duddingston (1778-1840) and also Hugh William Williams ('Grecian Williams') (1773-1829). McCulloch's technique is more akin to Dutch seventeenth century painting rather than the classical style. He revelled in painting the grandeur and wildness of the Highlands. His paintings were very popular, especially through the medium of engravings. Yet he was virtually unknown outside Scotland; he never travelled abroad. He exhibited mainly at the Royal Scottish Academy, sending only two pictures to the Royal Academy. He was elected ARSA in 1834 and RSA in 1838, the year he settled in Edinburgh.

McNEIL MACLEAY, ARSA

?-1848

Little is known about the life of Macleay other than that he was the brother of Kenneth Macleay (1802-1878), the portrait and figure painter who was one of the Foundation Members of the Royal Scottish Academy. It is known that McNeil Macleay settled in Edinburgh, and was elected ARSA in 1836. He withdrew from the Royal Scottish Academy in 1848 when, shortly before his death, he moved to Stirling.

Macleay exhibited only one picture at the Royal Academy in London (in 1839): 'View near the Head of Loch Eil, Inverness-shire'. Flemings' 'Head of Loch Eil' is dated 1840.

WILLIAM McTAGGART, RSA, RSW

1835-1910

McTaggart was born near Campbeltown in Argyll, the son of a crofter. At 16 he left for Glasgow to develop his natural gift for drawing. Sir Daniel Macnee advised him to enrol at the Trustees' Academy in Edinburgh, which had just appointed Robert Scott Lauder as its Director. McTaggart supported himself by accepting portrait commissions both whilst a student and later when he married and had a large family. However, as soon as he felt financially secure, he concentrated on landscape and seascape. He excelled at painting the sea and shore and from 1876 returned every summer to paint at Machrihanish near Campbeltown. He also painted on the East Coast, especially at Carnoustie. In 1889 he settled at Broomieknowe in Midlothian, where he remained for the rest of his life. His early work was influenced somewhat by the Pre-Raphaelites but gradually his technique became looser and he developed an impressionist style, apparently unaware of similar trends on the Continent. His later painting can be described as almost expressionist. He was elected ARSA in 1859, when only 24, and RSA in 1870. He was Vice President of the Royal Scottish Society of Painters in Water-colours from its formation in 1878 and Vice President of the Society of Scottish Artists from 1899.

JOHN WATSON NICOL

?-1926

Little is known about the life of Nicol. He was the son of Erskine Nicol (1825-1904), the genre painter, and brother of Erskine E Nicol, who was also a painter. It seems probable that he was born in Edinburgh, but he was brought up in London, following his father's move there in 1863. Watson Nicol painted historical and genre subjects and portraits. He was influenced by John Pettie. He exhibited at the Royal Academy in London and elsewhere from 1876 to 1924.

'Lochaber No More', the tragedy of a Highlander forced to leave his homeland, was exhibited at the Royal Academy in 1883 (No.611) and illustrated in The Art Journal of 1884.

WALLER HUGH PATON, RSA, RSW

1828-1895

Paton was born in Dunfermline, where his father was a damask designer. He was the brother of Sir Joseph Noel Paton (1821-1901), who declined the Presidency of the Royal Scottish Academy in 1891, and of Mrs D O Hill, the sculptor and wife of the photographer and painter. Waller Paton was largely self-taught, although he did study landscape at the Trustees' Academy in Edinburgh for a short period. He was much influenced by the Pre-Raphaelites. He painted Highland landscapes in the main, achieving almost immediate success. In 1857, six years after first exhibiting at the Royal Scottish Academy, he was elected ARSA; he became an Academician in 1865.

MABEL PRYDE

1871-1918

Mabel Pryde was born in Edinburgh, where her father was a lecturer in English literature, and, latterly, headmaster of Edinburgh Ladies' College. She studied art at Bushey, the art school founded by Sir Hubert von Herkomer, and there she met and married William Nicholson, who was working with her brother James as the 'Beggarstaff Brothers', a partnership which revolutionised poster design. The Nicholsons both became highly successful painters of still-life and portraits, and their eldest son, Ben Nicholson (1894-1984), was destined to become one of the major twentieth century painters.

SIR GEORGE REID, PRSA, HRSW

1841-1913

Born in Aberdeen, Reid was an apprentice lithographer before he decided to concentrate on painting, enrolling at the Trustees' Academy in Edinburgh in 1862. In 1866 he studied in Utrecht with G A Mollinger, becoming a close friend of Josef Israels and other Hague School painters. This was followed by a year's study in Paris under Adolphe Yvon at the Ecole des Beaux-Arts. Returning to Aberdeen in 1869 he became established as a very successful and distinguished portrait painter, especially of men. He was also a painter of fine landscapes and delicate flower studies, as well as a very fine draughtsman in pen and ink. He moved permanently to Edinburgh in 1885. He was elected ARSA in 1870 and RSA in 1877 and became the seventh President of the Royal Scottish Academy in 1891, the year in which he was knighted; he retired as President in 1902.

TOM SCOTT, RSA

1854-1927

Born in Selkirk, Scott began work as a tailor with his father until, in 1877, he enrolled at the Trustees' Academy in Edinburgh. He exhibited at the Royal Scottish Academy from 1883, at first figure subjects and, later, Border landscapes, almost always in watercolours in which medium he was undoubtedly one of the most accomplished painters of his generation. He also painted in other parts of Scotland, Holland, Italy and North Africa. He was elected ARSA in 1888 and RSA in 1902.

WILLIAM PAGE ATKINSON WELLS

1872-1923

Born in Glasgow, Wells moved with his parents to Australia in 1885. He returned to London in 1890 to study art at the Slade School under Alphonse Legros. He continued his studies in Paris under Bouguereau and Ferrier. Wells was a landscape and figure painter. He lived for a time in Glasgow, then spent seven years as a scene painter in Preston, Lancashire, followed by ten years in the Isle of Man, before finally settling in Devon.

SIR DAVID WILKIE, RA

1785-1841

Born at Cults in Fife, the third son of the parish minister, Wilkie enrolled at the Trustees' Academy in Edinburgh when he was 14. In 1805 he moved to London, studying at the Royal Academy Schools. He was a pre-eminent genre painter with an exceptional gift for observation of character, his early work in the manner of Ostade and Teniers. He exhibited 'The Village Politicians' at the Royal Academy in 1806 and became an overnight success. Subsequently, he turned to historical genre and, later, to portraiture. His paintings attracted the widest popularity, especially through the medium of engravings. He was elected ARA in 1809, when only 24, and RA in 1811. He was appointed the King's Limner for Scotland in 1823 on the death of Raeburn, succeeded Lawrence as Painter in Ordinary to the King in 1830 and was knighted in 1836. Following a serious breakdown, he made an extended visit to the Continent during the period 1825-28, travelling to France, Italy, Germany and Spain. In 1840 he travelled to the Holy Land, but on the way back he became ill and died. He was buried at sea off Gibraltar, an occasion immortalised by Turner in his painting 'Peace, Burial at Sea'.

SIR JAMES LAWTON WINGATE, PRSA

1846-1924

Born near Glasgow, Wingate spent several years in a merchant's office before he was able to take up art full-time. In 1867 he spent six months in Italy where he began to paint en plein air. In 1872 he moved to Edinburgh and enrolled at the Trustees' Academy, joining the life class at the RSA Schools a year later. Essentially a pastoral painter, incidents of country life and labour enriched his landscapes. Latterly, sunsets had a particular fascination for him. He was elected ARSA in 1879 and RSA in 1886. He served as the ninth President of the Royal Scottish Academy from 1919 to 1923, being knighted in 1920.

John Knox
Milton House, Mill and Greenhill Farm, looking south west towards Dumbarton Rock (455)

15

Robert Hope
The Old Pier,

David Farquharson
Fresh Herring (349)

Sir David Wilkie
Study for 'Old Mortality'

Robert Weir Allan
The Return Home from
Fishing (380)

Robert McGown Coventry
The Harbour,

Charles Lees
*Skating on Duddingston
Loch (327)*

Mabel Pryde
*The Artist's Daughter,
Nancy, as Pierrot (287)*

Horatio McCulloch
*Distant View of the River
Clyde (324)*

Samuel Bough
*Bruce's Stone, Glen
Trool, Galloway* (2)

John Fleming
*Extensive View of the
Clyde from Dalnottar Hill*
(234)

Sir George Reid
A Quiet River Bed,

Sir James Lawton Wingate
The Village Bridge (399)

James Docharty
The Mill Dam,
Ardnaham (322)

John Henderson

*Scottish Coastal
Landscape, looking
towards the Bass*

William Alfred Gibson
The Islands from Morar
(450)

Thomas Faed
The Last of the Clan (43)

Flemings' picture is a study for "The Last of the
Clan" which was exhibited at the Royal Academy,
London in 1865, with the following narrative:
*"When the steamer had slowly backed out, and
John MacAlpine had thrown off the hawser, we
began to feel that our once powerful clan was
now represented by a feeble old man and his
grand-daughter; who, together with some
outlying kith-and-kin, myself among the number,
owned not a single blade of grass in the glen that
was once all our own."*

41

William McTaggart

The Barley Field,
Sandy Dean (155)

Tom Scott
Border Landscape (128)
Watercolour

The Glasgow School

During the final two decades of the nineteenth century Glasgow was nearing the peak of its industrial and commercial prosperity and confidence, culminating in two International Exhibitions in 1888 and 1901. During the same period there was a remarkable flowering of painting in Glasgow. The city became the base for a group of young artists who later gained renown throughout Europe and North America as the Glasgow Boys. They were stimulated by the painting of Jules Bastien-Lepage, Courbet, the Hague School and the Barbizon artists. The work of these Continental painters was being brought to Glasgow by dealers such as Craibe Angus and, later, Alexander Reid and bought by several wealthy Glasgow industrialist collectors. The young Scottish artists shared an enthusiasm for realism and painting en plein air. Their work was characterised by a vigorous handling of paint and bold use of colour. The Glasgow Boys rejected the academic values of the artistic Establishment and its highly finished sentimental and anecdotal paintings. They resented the attitudes of the Royal Scottish Academy – they protested that artists would seem to have to live in Edinburgh before the Academy would consider them or hang their work.

Although there is some argument about who should be included in the group – it has been suggested that there were twenty-three artists in all – there is no disagreement about who were the leading members:

Joseph Crawhall (qv)

Thomas Millie Dow (1848-1919)

David Gauld (qv)

Sir James Guthrie (1859-1930)

George Henry (qv)

Edward Atkinson Hornel (1864-1933)

William Kennedy (1859-1918)

Sir John Lavery (qv)

William York Macgregor (qv)

Arthur Melville (qv)

J Stuart Park (1862-1933)

James Paterson (qv)

Alexander Roche (1861-1921)

Robert Macaulay Stevenson (1854-1952)

Edward Arthur Walton (qv)

They were a loose-knit company of artists, tending to paint in groups (for example, Macgregor and Paterson; Guthrie, Walton, Crawhall and, later, Henry). They did not all live in Glasgow at the same time, but at various times used or visited studios in that city. The artists congregated in the winter at Macgregor's studio in Bath Street, which bore the nearest resemblance to a Paris atelier to be found in Scotland. They travelled widely, painting at various locations in Scotland and England and abroad in France, Spain, the Mediterranean, the Middle East and Japan.

International recognition came in 1890, when the group's work was shown at the Grosvenor Gallery in London and, later that year, in Munich. Successful exhibitions followed in, for example, Berlin, Vienna, Chicago, Philadelphia and New York and their work was purchased by a growing number of art galleries abroad.

By 1900, however, the original vitality had run out. Several of the artists had left Glasgow for good. More were to follow, mainly to London, where they concentrated on the more lucrative business of portrait painting. The majority of the leading figures were to become members of the very Establishment that they had once despised. But their painting, particularly during the period 1880-95, regenerated Scottish art and was to have a strong influence on the next generation of Scottish artists.

Artists represented

SIR DAVID YOUNG CAMERON, RA, RSA, RWS, RSW

1865-1945

Born in Glasgow, Cameron embarked on what was to be a short and unhappy period in business, attending Glasgow School of Art in his spare time. In 1885 he gave up business, moved to Edinburgh and started full-time training at the Life School of the Royal Scottish Academy. Subsequently, he built up a considerable reputation as a landscape artist in oils and watercolours and especially as a brilliant etcher. He was elected ARSA in 1904, ARA in 1916, RSA in 1918 and RA in 1920. He was knighted in 1924 and appointed His Majesty's Painter & Limner in Scotland in 1933.

JOSEPH CRAWHALL, RSW

1861-1913

Born in Morpeth, Crawhall was taught to draw from memory by his father, a well-to-do rope manufacturer and amateur artist. He had no formal art training except for a period of two months at Atelier Aimé Morot in Paris in 1882. He was a leading member of the Glasgow School, having met E A Walton in 1879 (Walton's architect brother, Richard, was married to Crawhall's sister, Judith). Crawhill and Walton, along with James Guthrie, formed a lasting friendship. They spent several seasons together painting at Rosneath (near Helensburgh), Brig o'Turk and Cockburnspath, which has been described as the Barbizon of Scotland. Crawhall visited Morocco in 1884, returning there frequently during the next nine years. He was noted especially for his gouaches and watercolours of animals and birds. He was elected RSW in 1887, but resigned in 1893 and devoted a great deal of time to hunting!

DAVID GAULD, RSA

1865-1936

Born in Glasgow, Gauld appears to have studied part-time at Glasgow School of Art while working as an apprentice lithographer, before becoming an illustrator on the 'Glasgow Weekly Citizen'. He studied in Paris in 1889 and in 1896 painted at Grez-sur-Loing, a small French village to the south of Fontainebleau with a flourishing artists' colony. He was one of the younger members of the Glasgow School and became a close friend of Charles Rennie Mackintosh (1868-1928). His early work was influenced by Rossetti and bridged the gap between the Glasgow School and Art Nouveau although, later, he returned to the more usual Glasgow School style. He was a noted designer of stained-glass; his most important work was the design of stained-glass windows for St Andrew's Church in Buenos Aires, a commission which took almost ten years to complete. Thereafter, he resumed his painting and became well known for his pictures of cattle and calves. He was elected ARSA in 1918 and RSA in 1924. In 1935, a year before his death, he was appointed Director of Design Studies at Glasgow School of Art.

GEORGE HENRY, RA, RSA, RSW

1858-1943

Born in Ayrshire, Henry studied at Glasgow School of Art and attended informal life classes at the studio of W Y Macgregor in Glasgow. He was a leading member of the Glasgow School. He met James Guthrie, Joseph Crawhall and E A Walton in 1881 and painted with them at Rosneath, Brig o'Turk and, later, at Eyemouth and Cockburnspath. In 1885 he met E A Hornel and they became firm friends, sharing a studio and cooperating on a number of paintings. In 1889 Henry painted 'A Galloway Landscape' (Glasgow Art Gallery), which, although criticised at the time, is certainly one of the masterpieces of the Glasgow School. To convalesce from a serious illness he went to Japan accompanied by Hornel in 1892, which had a considerable influence on his future painting. Like a number of members of the Glasgow School, he eventually went to live in London and concentrated on portrait painting, gaining wide popularity and financial success. He was elected ARSA in 1892, RSA in 1902, ARA in 1907 and RA in 1920.

SIR JOHN LAVERY, RA, RSA, RHA

1856-1941

Born in Belfast, Lavery was orphaned at an early age and was brought up by relatives in Ulster and, later, in Ayrshire. A leading member of the Glasgow School, he studied at Glasgow School of Art, Heatherley's in London and Atelier Julian in Paris under Bouguereau. He was influenced by the work of Bastien-Lepage and along with other young artists painted en plein art at Grez-sur-Loing. Lavery returned to Glasgow in 1885 and that winter he completed his major work, 'The Tennis Party' (Aberdeen Art Gallery), which was exhibited at the Royal Academy in London in 1886 and in Munich in 1890, where it did much to establish the international reputation of the Glasgow Boys. In 1888 he was asked to record the visit of Queen Victoria to the Glasgow International Exhibition; this commission was to be the stepping stone to his future success and fame as an international society portrait painter. In 1890 he travelled to Morocco, returning there several times, finally establishing a winter retreat at Tangier. He moved permanently from Glasgow to London in 1896, where he associated with Whistler. He was elected ARSA in 1892, RSA in 1896, ARA in 1911 and RA in 1921; he was knighted in 1918.

WILLIAM YORK MACGREGOR, RSA, RSW

1855-1923

Born at Finnart, Dunbartonshire, the son of a Glasgow shipbuilder, Macgregor studied in Glasgow under Robert Greenlees and James Docherty and in London at the Slade under Alphonse Legros. He has been called 'the father of the Glasgow School'. Certainly the School's origins date from 1878, when along with James Paterson, his life-long friend, he painted at St. Andrews, Stonehaven and Nairn. Both continued to paint there during each summer up to 1881. He held informal life classes in his Glasgow studio at 134 Bath Street during the winters of 1881-84, which were attended by all the leading members of the Glasgow School except Guthrie and Melville. Macgregor's forceful, well-disciplined technique and direct approach to the subject was a strong influence on the other Glasgow Boys. In his later work he developed a brilliant colour sense which influenced future Scottish artists. His masterpiece, 'The Vegetable Stall' (National Gallery of Scotland), was painted in 1884. Asthma forced him to leave Glasgow in 1885 for Bridge of Allan and eventually South Africa, returning to Scotland in 1890. He was elected ARSA in 1898 and RSA in 1921.

ALEXANDER MANN

1853-1908

Born into a well-to-do Glasgow family, Mann was given every encouragement to develop his talent for art. He sketched while on family holidays abroad and, when he was apprenticed to his father's firm in 1870, he studied in the evenings at Glasgow School of Art. In 1877 he settled in Paris, studying at Atelier Julian and moving to the studio of Carolus-Duran in 1881. On a visit to Venice in 1884 he painted 'La Fileuse de Perles', which was exhibited at the Salon des Beaux Arts in Paris in 1885. The painting received an Honourable Mention, the first award of this kind received by a Glasgow-born artist. He was friendly with a number of members of the Glasgow School, particularly Millie Dow. In 1887 he married and settled in Berkshire, but he travelled extensively both at home and abroad, including Tangier where he and his family stayed from 1890 to 1892. Although of independent means, he worked hard to perfect his technique and exhibited regularly at home and in Paris.

ARTHUR MELVILLE, ARSA, RWS, RSW

1855-1904

Born at Loanhead of Guthrie, Angus, Melville was brought up at East Linton. Apprenticed at 15 to a local grocer, Melville made his way the eight miles to

Edinburgh and back each evening to attend art classes. He continued his evening classes when he became a book-keeper in Dalkeith, studying for two years with James Campbell Noble. In 1878 he decided to go to Paris, where he studied at Atelier Julian for two years. He visited Barbizon and Grez-sur-Loing, living and working at Grez during 1879. In the following year he set out alone for Egypt and the Middle East. His experiences and work on that journey formed the basis of his future reputation as a painter of oriental subjects, particularly in watercolour in which he developed an individual style which was to exert a strong influence on other Scottish artists. He returned to Scotland in 1882. Later he was to visit Tangier and Spain. Although he lived in Edinburgh, he was regarded by the Glasgow Boys as a member, being particularly friendly with James Guthrie and Joseph Crawhall. He travelled frequently to Glasgow to see the other members and painted with Guthrie at Cockburnspath and in Orkney. In 1889 he left Edinburgh and settled in London, although he often returned to Scotland to paint. In London, Melville became a popular and much respected figure in the art world, a friend of Whistler and a member of the Committee of the International Society. He was elected ARSA in 1886. He died of typhoid in 1904 at the peak of his powers.

JAMES PATERSON, RSA, PRSW, RWS

1854-1932

Paterson was born in Glasgow, the son of a prosperous cotton and muslin manufacturer. He started work as a clerk, studying in his spare time at Glasgow School of Art and attending watercolour classes given by A D Robertson. In 1878, his father eventually agreed to allow him to study art in Paris. He spent two winters in the studio of Jacquesson de la Chevreuse and three in that of Jean Paul Laurens, painting in Scotland and abroad during the summer. He was one of the leading members of the Glasgow School and a life-long friend of W Y Macgregor. Paterson was primarily a landscape painter. It was in 1879 that he first visited Moniaive in Dumfriesshire, where his finest works were painted. In 1884 he married and settled in Moniaive, although he still maintained some contact with what was happening in Glasgow. He was very much involved with the launch of 'The Scottish Art Review' in 1888, but it folded the following year. In 1890 he exhibited at Munich with the other members of the Glasgow School, gaining a 2nd Class Gold Medal for 'The Passing Storm'. From 1897 he maintained a studio in Edinburgh, moving there permanently in 1906. He was elected ARSA in 1896 and RSA in 1910. He acted as Librarian of the Royal Scottish Academy from 1910 to 1924 and Secretary from 1924 to 1931. From 1922 to 1932 he was also President of the Royal Scottish Society of Painters in Water-colours.

EDWARD ARTHUR WALTON, RSA, PRSW

1860-1922

Born at Glanderston House, Renfrewshire, Walton studied at Dusseldorf Academy and Glasgow School of Art. He was a leading member of the Glasgow School. While still in their teens, Walton, James Guthrie and Joseph Crawhall formed a close and lasting friendship, painting together at Rosneath, Brig o'Turk, Cockburnspath and in Lincolnshire. A landscape painter by inclination, he was well known also as a portrait painter. He was elected ARSA in 1889. The same year he visited Paris with Guthrie, Arthur Melville and John Singer Sargent. He spent a period in London between 1893 and 1904, when he

associated with Whistler – it was said that Walton was the only man with whom Whistler never quarrelled. Family summer holidays were spent painting around Wenhaston in Suffolk, a practice which continued after his return to Edinburgh in 1905, the year he was elected RSA. He renewed his friendship with Guthrie, who was now the President of the Royal Scottish Academy, and the two painters visited Algiers and Spain together in 1907 and Brussels and Ghent in 1913. Latterly, Galloway became Walton's favourite painting ground. He served as President of the Royal Scottish Society of Painters in Water-colours from 1915 to his death in 1922.

David Gauld

A Breton Village (413)

Alexander Mann
Sand Dunes, Tangier
(427)

Sir D Y Cameron
The Tweed (404)
Watercolour

Sir D Y Cameron
Loch Lubnaig,
Perthshire (478)

William York Macgregor
Near St. Andrews (406)

W Y Macgregor

James Paterson
Edinburgh from

Arthur Melville
Pangbourne (222)
Watercolour

Joseph Crawhall
The Bull Ring, Algeciras (377)
Watercolour

Edward Arthur Walton

Edward Arthur Walton
The Willows (416)

Edward Arthur Walton
Back Wynd, Ceres (411)

FOLLOWING PAGE
George Henry
Girl Reading (228)
Pastel

GEORGE HENRY.
1896.

66

The Scottish Colourists

S J Peploe, Leslie Hunter and F C B Cadell comprise the group known as the Scottish Colourists. J D Fergusson also may be included, although he is often omitted because he spent so much of his life in France. Their painting developed in an artistic environment dominated at home by William McTaggart and the Glasgow School and abroad by the Impressionists and Post-Impressionists. All were attracted by the lively artistic life of Paris, spending varying periods in that city. At that time the post-impressionism of Cezanne, Van Gogh and Gauguin was giving way to Matisse and the Fauves, only to be quickly followed by Picasso and the Cubists. The Paris of the Third Republic acted as a magnet for artists from many countries, thronging the studios, streets and cafes of Montparnasse. In the period before the First World War artists such as Matisse, Derain, Bonnard, Vuillard, Modigliani, Picasso and Chagall worked in Paris. For Fergusson, Peploe and Cadell it must have been a revelation indeed to experience Parisian life and art after the staid, Calvinistic atmosphere of Edinburgh. The work of the Impressionists could be seen in the Salle Caillebotte and the gallery of Durand-Ruel. There were the Van Gogh and Cezanne retrospective exhibitions in 1901 and 1907 respectively and the Whistler memorial exhibition in 1905, as well as the Salons. Another dimension was added by the arrival in 1909 of Diaghilev and the Ballets Russes, which so exhilarated Peploe and Fergusson.

The Scottish Colourists did not develop as a group, but pursued independent careers. Indeed, the descriptive name was not coined until 1948, when only Fergusson was still alive. Their painting developed at varying rates, passing through different stages. In most respects, Fergusson was the pioneer of the four. All used colour in a high key. All at one time or another were attracted by the brilliant light of the South of France and spent some time painting on the Cote d'Azur and further west at Cassis. Occasionally two of the group painted together – for example, in Paris Fergusson and Peploe belonged to a circle of foreign painters and over a number of years painted together at Paris-Plage, Royan (near Bordeaux) and in the South of France. They were all somewhat contrasting characters. Peploe was shy and retiring; Cadell was an extrovert, perhaps a little eccentric; Fergusson was very precise in dress – he did not look like an artist – his studio was very clean and ordered; Hunter was Bohemian in appearance and was somewhat disorganised. Individually encouraged in their early careers by the dealers Alexander Reid in Glasgow and Aitken Dott in Edinburgh, it was not until 1923 that Peploe, Cadell and Hunter

had a joint exhibition at The Leicester Galleries in London. This was followed in 1924 by a group exhibition at the Galerie Barbazanges in Paris. Subsequent group exhibitions were held in Scotland, London and, in 1931, at the Galeries Georges Petit in Paris when, on that occasion, the group was joined by Telfer Bear and R O Dunlop.

Unlike the majority of the Glasgow School, the later works of the Colourists are as good or better than their early paintings. Their art had a considerable influence on the development of subsequent Scottish painting.

Artists represented

FRANCIS CAMPBELL BOILEAU CADELL, RSA, RSW

1883-1937

Born in Edinburgh, Cadell studied at the RSA Schools before going to Paris in 1899, accompanied by his mother and sister. It was Arthur Melville, a close friend of Cadell's father, who had suggested that Cadell train in Paris. His first picture was hung in the Salon when he was 16. Apart from a short period in Munich, he spent the next eight years in Paris, studying at Atelier Julian from 1899 to 1903, returning to Edinburgh in 1909. He made an extended, revelatory visit to Venice in 1910. His early work was influenced by McTaggart and Whistler and included still-lifes and stylish drawing room interiors. In 1913 he visited Iona, returning each year to paint there for almost 20 years. The landscapes he painted there were marked by the use of great intensity of colour. In 1920 he painted at Cassis in the South of France. Matisse and the Fauves influenced his later work, particularly the many paintings of the interior of his Edinburgh flat which he executed in the 1920's and 1930's. He was elected ARSA in 1931 and RSA in 1936. He was a founder and life-long member of the Society of Eight.

JOHN DUNCAN FERGUSSON

1874-1961

Born in Leith, Fergusson decided against training as a naval surgeon to take up painting, renting a studio in Edinburgh in 1894. He had no formal art training, although he did attend classes for a short time at Atelier Colarossi in Paris in the late 1890's. His first visit to Paris was probably in 1896. He returned regularly, as well as visiting Morocco and Spain, until 1907 when he decided to settle in

Paris, becoming one of the principal members of a circle of Anglo-American artists in Paris. He met some of the leading figures of the avant-garde, exhibited at the Salon d'Automne and taught part-time at Academie de la Palette, where he formed a friendship with Segonzac, and, later, at Atelier Blanche. Fergusson acknowledged the early influence of Arthur Melville; later he was influenced by Matisse and the Fauves and became friendly with Friesz. In 1906 he had met Anne Estelle Rice, the American artist, with whom he developed a close relationship, she providing the inspiration for many of his pictures. He cooperated with Middleton Murry and Katherine Mansfield in the launch of the magazine 'Rhythm'. In 1913 he met Margaret Morris, the dancer and founder of the international Margaret Morris Movement, whom later he was to marry. In the meantime he had moved to the South of France, returning to London on the outbreak of war in 1914. In 1929 he settled for a second time in Paris, making regular painting visits to Antibes. In 1939 he left Paris for Glasgow, where he lived for the rest of his long, fruitful life, continuing his annual visits to the South of France during the period 1950 to 1960.

GEORGE LESLIE HUNTER

1877-1931

Born at Rothesay, Hunter emigrated with his family to California when he was 13. He worked as a book and magazine illustrator, but decided to become a painter following a visit to Paris in 1904. He was largely self-taught. His first one-man exhibition had been due to open in San Francisco the day after the 1906 earthquake – all his pictures were destroyed. He returned to Glasgow and was compelled to resume his early career as a book and magazine illustrator. He continued painting, visiting France a number of times. His work came to the attention of Alexander Reid, who mounted a number of one-man exhibitions throughout his career. Hunter was influenced by a number of artists, including McTaggart, Whistler, Cezanne, and the Fauves. In 1922 he made an extended visit to the Continent – Paris, Venice, Florence and the French Riviera, where he saw a good deal of J D Fergusson. During the period 1924-27 he painted mainly in Scotland, including Fife and Loch Lomond; it was at Loch Lomond some six years later that he executed some of his finest paintings. From 1927 to 1929 he worked in the South of France. An unsuccessful London one-man exhibition in 1928 was followed by a noteworthy exhibition in New York in 1929 and a very successful group exhibition in Paris in 1931.

SAMUEL JOHN PEPLOE, RSA

1871-1935

Born in Edinburgh, Peploe decided against a career in law and took up art. He trained at Edinburgh College of Art and in Paris at Atelier Julian under Bouguereau and later at Atelier Colarossi. Except for the period 1910-12, when, following his marriage, he settled in Paris, he lived in Edinburgh, occupying studios at various addresses. He painted at many locations in Scotland, such as Barra, North Berwick, Comrie, Islay (with J D Fergusson), Arran and Kirkcudbright, and in France, usually with J D Fergusson, in Brittany, Royan, Cassis and Antibes. Encouraged by Cadell, in 1920 Peploe visited and found sanctuary in Iona. He returned there to paint almost every year for the next 13 years. His painting was influenced strongly by French artists, particularly Manet, Cezanne and Chabaud. He was elected ARSA in 1917 and RSA in 1927.

George Leslie Hunter
Loch Lomond (183)

George Leslie Hunter
Street In Villefranche
(336)
Pen & ink and crayon

Samuel John Peploe
Green Sea, Iona (179)

Samuel John Peploe
*The Luxembourg
Gardens (480)*

Samuel John Peploe
Still Life (28)

Francis Campbell Boileau Cadell
Loch Creran, Argyll (69)

Francis Campbell Boileau Cadell
The 'Dunara Castle' (70)

Francis Campbell
Boileau Cadell
Carnations (181)

Francis Campbell Boileau Cadell
Roses (330)
Watercolour

The Twentieth Century

At the turn of the century Scottish painting was flourishing. Scott Lauder's two foremost pupils, McTaggart in Scotland and Orchardson in London, continued to paint until the end of the first decade of the twentieth century. Although the artists of the Glasgow School had dispersed and their early crusading zeal had abated somewhat, their achievement was considerable and they were to exert a significant influence on the next generation of Scottish painters; indeed a number of them painted well into the present century. The Scottish Colourists were just beginning their careers and were to produce some of the best painting in Scotland over the next thirty years or so.

The applied arts too were flourishing. In the final decade of the nineteenth century and the first decade or so of the twentieth century the 'Glasgow Style', Scotland's distinctive version of Art Nouveau, was pioneered by 'The Four' – Charles Rennie Mackintosh (1868-1928) and his wife Margaret Macdonald (1864-1933), and James Herbert MacNair (1868-1955) and his wife Frances Macdonald (1873-1921) – along with Talwin Morris (1865-1911), Jessie Newbery (1864-1948), James Salmon (1873-1924) and George Walton (1867-1933), the brother of E A Walton (qv). Mackintosh trained as an architect and is now best known for his remarkable design of the new building for Glasgow School of Art, which was completed in 1909. But he also designed furniture and advised on interior decoration. George Walton and he collaborated on the striking designs of furniture, fittings and decor for two of Kate Cranston's tea-rooms in Glasgow, others being designed by Mackintosh himself. Later Mackintosh designed textiles and towards the end of his life concentrated on painting landscape in watercolours. Although acclaimed throughout Continental Europe, particularly at exhibitions in Vienna in 1900 and Turin in 1902, the Glasgow Style was not well received in London and met with less than enthusiasm in Glasgow itself. Indeed, the nickname 'The Spook School' was applied to The Four. The Glasgow Style was relatively short-lived and had no true sequel. A number of the designers, including Mackintosh, left Glasgow and harsher economic conditions and a renewed emphasis on traditional values resulted in its virtual demise in the early 1920's. Other Scottish exponents of Art Nouveau and Symbolism included Robert Burns (1869-1941) in Edinburgh and John Duncan (1866-1945) and George Dutch Davidson (1879-1901) in Dundee.

A feature of the opening decades of the twentieth century was the formation in Edinburgh and Glasgow of a number of small exhibition societies. The Society of Scottish Artists, which had been established in Edinburgh in 1891, not only provided an additional opportunity to exhibit, independent of the Royal Scottish Academy, but also mounted loan exhibitions, which included the important shows of the work of the Post-Impressionists in 1913 and of Edvard Munch in 1931; the Society still pursues its original aims. The Society of Eight was formed in Edinburgh in 1912; its founder-members were Patrick William Adam (1854-1929), David Alison (qv), F C B Cadell (qv), James Cadenhead (1858-1927), James Paterson (qv), Harrington Mann (1864-1937), John Lavery (qv) and Alexander Sinclair (1859-1930). An Edinburgh Group existed from 1912 to 1913 and from 1919 to 1921 and The Glasgow Society of Painters and Sculptors for a short time from 1919. The 1922 Group was founded by students who graduated that year from Edinburgh College of Art and included William Gillies (qv) and William MacTaggart (qv). Another characteristic of the present century, no doubt due to the changing economic climate, is that the majority of Scottish artists combine painting with the security of a teaching post at one of the four art schools: Gray's School of Art in Aberdeen, Duncan of Jordanstone College of Art in Dundee, Edinburgh College of Art and Glasgow School of Art.

Apart from the Colourists, a number of other Scottish painters came into prominence in the first half of the twentieth century. One of the most outstanding was the Glasgow artist John Quinton Pringle (1864-1925). An optician by profession, Pringle had attended evening classes in art held by the School Board of Glasgow and at Glasgow School of Art, where he was a fellow student of Mackintosh. He painted in his spare time, especially scenes of Glasgow streets and tenement courts, children and portrait miniatures. Other noteworthy artists include Stanley Cursiter (qv), the three Glasgow-trained artists James Cowie (1886-1956), who became the influential head of Hospitalfield House, Arbroath (which before the Second World War was a private art school, but now has only a post-graduate course), Robert Sivell (1888-1958) and Archibald McGlashan (born 1888), and the two Scottish-trained but London-based abstract artists William McCance (1894-1970) and William Johnstone (born 1894).

The successors to the Colourists were the artists now known as the Edinburgh School (although these artists regarded themselves as individuals rather than a group). The leading members were William Gillies, William MacTaggart, John Maxwell (1905-1962) and Anne Redpath (qv). All four had been students together at Edinburgh College of Art and all later joined the College's teaching staff; all had spent varying periods in France. Their subjects are mostly landscape and still-life and they are noted for their use of rich colour and their vigorous handling of paint. Other noteworthy artists of the middle decades of the century included the Glasgow-trained but London-based artists Robert MacBryde (1913-1966) and Robert Colquhoun (1914-1962), and also Robert Henderson Blyth (qv) and Joan Eardley (qv).

Living Scottish artists represented in the Flemings' collection include Mardi Barrie, Elizabeth Blackadder and her husband John Houston, John Gardner Crawford, David Donaldson, James Fairgrieve, David McClure, David Michie, James Morrison, Alberto Morrocco, James McIntosh Patrick and Robin Philipson (all qv).

Artists represented

DAVID ALISON, RSA, RP

1882-1955

Born at Dysart in Fife, Alison studied at Glasgow School of Art and in Paris and Italy. He joined the teaching staff of Edinburgh College of Art in 1913, retiring as Head of the School of Drawing and Painting at the College in 1946, when he moved to London. He painted mainly portraits and interiors. He was a founder-member of the Society of Eight and was elected ARSA in 1916 and RSA in 1922.

MARY ARMOUR, RSA, RSW

Born 1902

Born at Blantyre in Lanarkshire, Mary Armour studied at Glasgow School of Art from 1920 to 1925. She taught art in schools in Cambuslang and Glasgow until 1927, when she had to resign following her marriage to fellow artist William Armour, RSA, RSW (1903-1979). From 1951 to 1962 she was on the teaching staff of Glasgow School of Art. Her subjects are mainly still-life and landscapes. She was elected ARSA in 1941 and RSA in 1958.

ERIC AULD

Born 1931

Born in Aberdeen, Auld studied at Gray's School of Art from 1948 to 1953. Awarded a travelling scholarship in 1953, he visited France, Spain, Holland and Italy. Following a period teaching art at Aberdeen Academy, he is now Principal Teacher of Art at Kincorth Academy, Aberdeen.

MARDI BARRIE, RSW

Born 1931

Born and educated at Kirkcaldy in Fife, Mardi Barrie studied at the University of Edinburgh and Edinburgh College of Art from 1948 to 1953. After graduating, she took up her present teaching post at Broughton High School, Edinburgh. She was elected RSW in 1968.

ELIZABETH BLACKADDER, RA, RSA, RSW

Born 1931

Born in Falkirk, Elizabeth Blackadder studied at the University of Edinburgh and Edinburgh College of Art. Awarded travelling scholarships in 1954 and 1955, she visited Yugoslavia, Greece and Italy. In 1956 she married fellow artist John Houston (qv). Since 1962 she has been on the teaching staff of Edinburgh College of Art. She has travelled extensively in Europe and, in 1969, visited the United States of America. She was elected ARSA and RSA in 1963 and 1972 respectively and ARA and RA in 1971 and 1976 respectively, the first woman to be elected an Academician of both the Royal Academy and the Royal Scottish Academy. She is a Trustee of the National Galleries of Scotland.

ROBERT HENDERSON BLYTH, RSA, RSW

1919-1971

Born in Glasgow, Blyth had a picture exhibited at the Royal Scottish Academy when he was only 15. He studied at Glasgow School of Art from 1934 to 1939 and spent a post-Diploma year at Hospitalfield House in Arbroath under James Cowie, who was a considerable early influence on Blyth. In 1941 he joined the Army as a medical orderly and saw service in France, Belgium, Holland and Germany. He joined the teaching staff of Edinburgh College of Art in 1946 as an assistant to William Gillies, whom he accompanied on several painting expeditions in Scotland. In 1954 he left the College for Gray's School of Art in Aberdeen, being appointed Head of the Department of Drawing and Painting in 1960. He was elected ARSA in 1949 and RSA in 1958.

SIR DAVID MUIRHEAD BONE, HRSA

1876-1953

Born in Glasgow, the son of a journalist, Bone studied at evening classes at Glasgow School of Art and under Archibald Kay, RSA (1860-1935), while apprenticed to an architect for three years. In 1901 he moved to London, becoming a member of the New English Art Club and the Society of Twelve. He was a print-maker and etcher of distinction. In 1903 he married Gertrude Dodd, the sister of artist Francis Dodd. The Bones travelled extensively on the Continent and lived for some years in Italy and Spain. He was the first Official War Artist and worked on the Western Front and with the Fleet from 1916 to 1918 and for the Admiralty from 1940 to 1943. He was a Trustee of the National Gallery, the Tate Gallery and the Imperial War Museum. He was elected an Honorary RSA in 1951.

JOHN GARDINER CRAWFORD, RSW, RI

Born 1941

Born at Broadsea, Fraserburgh, Crawford studied at Gray's School of Art in

Aberdeen, in Paris and at Hospitalfield House, Arbroath from 1959 to 1964. After a year at Aberdeen College of Education, he taught in Aberdeenshire schools until 1972, when he joined Dundee College of Art as a lecturer in art. In 1980 he gave up his post at the College to concentrate full-time on painting, except for acting as artist-tutor at Newbattle Abbey College in Midlothian each summer. He was elected RSW in 1974. He is also a member of the Royal Society of British Artists and the Royal Institute of Painters in Water Colours.

VICTORIA CROWE

Born 1946

Born at Kingston-upon-Thames, Victoria Crowe studied at Kingston College of Art and the Royal College of Art in London from 1961 to 1968. She joined the teaching staff of Edinburgh College of Art in 1968 and since 1970 has lectured part-time at the College. She has executed a number of commissions for the Scottish National Portrait Gallery. She is a member of the Society of Scottish Artists.

STANLEY CURSITER, RSA, RSW

1887-1976

Born at Kirkwall, Cursiter studied at Edinburgh College of Art. From 1924 to 1930 he was Keeper of Art at the National Gallery of Scotland and in 1930 was appointed Director of the National Galleries of Scotland, a post he held until 1948. He was elected ARSA in 1927 and RSA in 1937, acting as the twelfth Secretary of the Academy from 1953 to 1955. In 1948 he was appointed His Majesty's Painter and Limner in Scotland. Cursiter lived most of his life in Edinburgh, but returned to his native Orkney towards the end of his life, being made Deputy Lieutenant of Orkney in 1971.

DAVID DONALDSON, RSA, RP

Born 1916

Born at Chryston in Lanarkshire, Donaldson was brought up in Coatbridge and studied at Glasgow School of Art from 1932 to 1937. Awarded a travelling scholarship, he visited Florence and Paris. After an additional year's study at Glasgow School of Art in 1938 he joined the teaching staff of the School on a part-time basis. He was appointed a full-time lecturer in 1944 and became Head of the Department of Drawing and Painting in 1967, retiring in 1981. He is best known as a portrait painter. He was elected ARSA and RSA in 1951 and 1962 respectively and a member of the Royal Society of Portrait Painters in 1964. He was appointed Her Majesty's Painter and Limner in Scotland in 1977.

JOAN EARDLEY, RSA

1921-1963

Born of Anglo-Scottish parents at Warnham in Sussex, Joan Eardley was brought up in Lincoln and London. On leaving school in 1938, she enrolled at Goldsmiths' School of Art, but stayed only one or two terms. At the beginning of the Second World War her family moved to Glasgow and she began studies at Glasgow School of Art under Hugh Adam Crawford. In 1943 she took a war-time job as a joiner's labourer. She resumed her studies in 1947 at Hospitalfield

House, Arbroath and then at Glasgow School of Art. Awarded a travelling scholarship, she visited Paris, Venice, Florence, Siena and Rome in 1948-9. Although she always maintained a studio in Glasgow, she painted at Corrie on Arran for some years and then at Catterline, south of Stonehaven on the East Coast, as well as occasionally visiting Caverslea in the Ettrick Valley in the Borders. She is particularly noted for her pictures of Glasgow's deprived children and, later, her elemental landscapes and seascapes. She was elected ARSA in 1955 and RSA in 1963. Joan Eardley died in 1963, after a serious illness, when she was only 42.

JAMES FAIRGRIEVE, ARSA, RSW

Born 1944

Born at Prestonpans in East Lothian, Fairgrieve studied at Edinburgh College of Art from 1962 to 1968. Awarded a travelling scholarship, he spent six months in Italy in 1969. He is on the teaching staff at Edinburgh College of Art. He was elected ARSA and RSW in 1975 and was President of the Society of Scottish Artists in 1978.

WILLIAM MILLER FRAZER, RSA

1864-1961

Born at Scone in Perthshire, Frazer moved to Edinburgh in the early 1880's and studied at the RSA Schools. He was primarily a landscape painter. He was elected ARSA in 1909 and RSA in 1924, serving as fourteenth Treasurer of the Academy from 1932 to 1938. Frazer holds the record for seventy-three consecutive years exhibiting at the Royal Scottish Academy. He was a founder-member of the Society of Scottish Artists and was elected President in 1908.

SIR WILLIAM GEORGE GILLIES, RA, RSA, PRSW

1898-1973

Born at Haddington in East Lothian, Gillies' studies at Edinburgh College of Art from 1916 to 1922 were interrupted by two years' war service in France. He was awarded a travelling scholarship in 1924 and studied in Paris under Andre Lhote, as well as visiting Venice and Florence. After a year teaching art at Inverness Academy, in 1926 he took up a part-time appointment at Edinburgh College of Art as assistant to David Alison (qv). Gillies became Head of the School of Painting at the College in 1946 and was Principal of the College from 1960 to 1966. From 1939 until his death he lived at Temple, Midlothian. He painted landscape and still-life. William McTaggart was an early influence; Gillies acknowledged the influence also of Gauguin, Bonnard, Matisse, Munch and Braque. He was a founder-member of the 1922 Group, was elected to the Society of Eight in 1932 and a member of the Society of Scottish Artists in 1937. He was elected ARSA and RSA in 1940 and 1947 respectively, and ARA and RA in 1964 and 1971 respectively. In 1963 he was elected President of the Royal Scottish Society of Painters in Water-colours. He was knighted in 1970.

GEORGE HOUSTON, RSA, RSW, RI

1869-1947

Born at Dalry in Ayrshire, Houston trained as a linoleum designer and lithographer in Glasgow. He worked as an illustrator for 'The Glasgow Evening Citizen' before he took up landscape painting and etching. He painted mainly in Ayrshire and Argyllshire. He visited Japan in 1911. He was elected ARSA in 1909 and RSA in 1924 and was also a member of the Royal Institute of Painters in Water Colours and the Society of 25 in London

IAN HOUSTON

Born 1934

Born at Gravesend in Kent, Houston studied both music and painting. After leaving the Royal College of Music in London, he taught music before concentrating on painting. He has lived in Norfolk since 1964, but spends part of his time on his sailing barge 'Raybel'. A marine and landscape artist, Houston is best known for his East Anglian and Continental port scenes.

JOHN HOUSTON, RSA, RSW

Born 1930

Born at Buckhaven in Fife, Houston studied at Edinburgh College of Art and Moray House College of Education. Awarded a travelling scholarship, he spent six months in Italy with David Michie (qv) in 1953-4. Since 1955 he has been on the teaching staff at Edinburgh College of Art. In 1956 he married Elizabeth Blackadder (qv). In 1972 he visited Racine (USA) on a Johnson & Johnson travelling scholarship. He was elected ARSA in 1964 and RSA in 1972, serving as Librarian of the Royal Scottish Academy from 1972 to 1982.

DOROTHY JOHNSTONE, ARSA

1892-1980

Born in Edinburgh, Dorothy Johnstone was the daughter of the landscape painter George Whitton Johnstone (1849-1901). She studied at Edinburgh College of Art and joined the staff of the College in 1914. In 1915 she made the first of many visits to the artists' colony at Kirkcudbright. She was very friendly with fellow artists Cecile Walton (1891-1956), the daughter of the Glasgow School painter E A Walton (qv), and Eric Robertson (1887-1941). All were members of the Edinburgh Group and exhibited at the Group's exhibitions in 1919-21. In 1924 she married David McBeth Sutherland (1883-1973), another member of the re-formed Edinburgh Group. After marriage she had to give up her teaching post at Edinburgh College of Art, but she continued to paint. She was elected ARSA in 1962.

HENRY JOHN LINTOTT, RSA

1877-1965

Born at Brighton, Lintott studied at Brighton College of Art, the Royal College of Art in London and in Paris and Italy. Around 1902 he joined the teaching staff of the Royal Institution Schools in Edinburgh, shortly to be reconstituted as Edinburgh College of Art. He painted mostly portraits and figure subjects. He was elected ARSA in 1916 and RSA in 1923.

JAMES McBEY

1883-1959

Born at Newburgh on the Aberdeenshire coast, McBey joined the North of Scotland Bank in Aberdeen in 1899, but resigned in 1910 to concentrate on etching. He was largely self-taught, although he had taken private art lessons

and attended evening classes at Gray's School of Art in Aberdeen while employed by the Bank. He moved to London in 1911. His first exhibition of etchings at Goupil's was a great success and thereafter he gained a very considerable reputation as an etcher and watercolourist. He was appointed an Official War Artist to the Egyptian Expeditionary Force from 1917 to 1918. He travelled extensively throughout his life, visiting Spain, Morocco, Italy, USA and France. At the outbreak of the Second World War he was in the USA and he stayed there until 1946, taking US citizenship in 1942. During the latter part of his life he resided in Morocco, where he continued to paint, dying at Tangier in 1959.

DAVID McCLURE, RSA, RSW

Born 1926

Born at Lochwinnoch in Renfrewshire, where his father was a furniture designer, McClure's studies at the University of Glasgow were interrupted in 1944 by war service in the mines. Thereafter, he studied fine art at the University of Edinburgh and Edinburgh College of Art. The award of scholarships took him to Spain and Italy in 1952-3, after which he taught part-time at Edinburgh College of Art, being awarded the Andrew Grant Fellowship in 1955. He spent a period living in Sicily. In 1957 he joined the teaching staff of Duncan of Jordanstone College of Art in Dundee. He became Senior Lecturer in the School of Drawing and Painting at the College in 1971, retiring in 1985. He was elected ARSA in 1963 and RSA in 1971.

DONALD McINTYRE

Born 1923

Born in Yorkshire of Scottish parents, McIntyre was brought up in the north west of Scotland. He trained as a dentist in Glasgow, studying painting at evening classes at Glasgow School of Art and with James Wright, RSW at Garelochhead. He now lives in North Wales, having given up dentistry to concentrate full-time on landscape painting.

SIR WILLIAM MacTAGGART, PRSA, RA

1903-1980

MacTaggart, the son of a marine engineer and the grandson of William McTaggart (qv), the noted landscape and seascape painter, was born at Loanhead on the outskirts of Edinburgh and studied part-time at Edinburgh College of Art. During the period from 1923 to the outbreak of the Second World War he made annual visits to France, painting at various locations on the Mediterranean coast – his first one-man exhibition was held in the church hall of St. Andrew's Scottish Church in Cannes in 1924 when he was 21. After the War the visits to France were resumed, this time to a village just north of Paris. He taught part-time at Edinburgh College of Art from 1933 to 1956. He painted mainly still-life, landscape and, later, seascape. Artists who influenced MacTaggart's work included Cezanne, Segonzac, Matisse, Munch and Rouault. He was a founder-member of the 1922 Group and was elected a member of the Society of Scottish Artists in 1922 and to the Society of Eight in 1927. He was elected ARSA in 1937 and RSA in 1948, serving as Secretary of the Academy from 1955 to 1959 and fourteenth President from 1959 to 1969. He was knighted in 1962. He was elected ARA and RA in 1968 and 1973 respectively.

DAVID MICHIE, RSA

Born 1928

Born at St. Raphael on the Mediterranean coast of France, the son of Anne Redpath (qv), Michie studied at Edinburgh College of Art. He visited Italy on a travelling scholarship in 1953-4. He taught drawing and painting at Gray's School of Art in Aberdeen from 1957 to 1961, when he joined the teaching staff of Edinburgh College of Art. He is now Head of the School of Drawing and Painting at the College and was Vice-Principal from 1974 to 1977. Michie was President of the Society of Scottish Artists from 1961 to 1963 and was elected ARSA in 1964 and RSA in 1972.

JOHN MacLAUCHLAN MILNE, RSA

1886-1957

Born in Edinburgh, the son of the landscape painter Joseph Milne (1861-1911), Milne studied in Edinburgh and Paris. He lived in Dundee until 1929, when he moved to Arran. He concentrated on landscape painting and travelled extensively on the Continent, working especially in the South of France. He was elected ARSA in 1933 and RSA in 1937.

JAMES MORRISON, ARSA, RSW

Born 1932

Born in Glasgow, Morrison studied at Glasgow School of Art from 1950 to 1954. He taught part-time at the School until 1958, when he moved to Catterline on the Kincardineshire coast. He was visiting artist at Hospitalfield House in Arbroath in 1962-63. In 1965 he moved to Montrose and took up his present teaching post at Duncan of Jordanstone College of Art, Dundee. Awarded an Arts Council Travelling Scholarship, he visited Greece in 1968. He was elected RSW in 1970 and ARSA in 1973.

ALBERTO MORROCCO, RSA, RSW, RP

Born 1917

Born in Aberdeen of Italian parents, Morrocco studied at Gray's School of Art in Aberdeen from 1932 to 1938. Awarded two travelling scholarships, he visited France and Switzerland in 1939. Following Army service from 1940 to 1946, he taught part-time at Gray's. From 1950 to 1982 he was Head of Painting at Duncan of Jordanstone College of Art, Dundee. He was elected ARSA in 1951, RSA in 1962 and RSW in 1965. He has specialised in still-life, figure subjects and landscape, but is also a successful portrait painter.

JAMES McINTOSH PATRICK, RSA

Born 1907

Born in Dundee, the son of an architect, McIntosh Patrick studied at Glasgow School of Art where he won the Newbery Prize. He started as an etcher in 1927, on contract for £250 a year to produce twelve plates, but with the collapse of the etching market during the Depression, he turned to oils and watercolours. He had early success, with pictures acquired for many public galleries including the Tate Gallery. He still lives and works in Dundee, enjoying wide popularity for his local views. He has also painted portraits. He was elected ARSA in 1949 and

RSA in 1957 and is also an Associate of the Royal Society of Painter-Etchers and a Member of the Royal Institute of Painters in Oil Colours.

SIR ROBIN PHILIPSON, PRSA, RA, RSW

Born 1916

Born at Broughton-in-Furness in Lancashire, Philipson was educated in Whitehaven and Dumfries and studied at Edinburgh College of Art from 1936 to 1940. After service in India and Burma during the Second World War and a short period of teacher training, he joined the teaching staff of Edinburgh College of Art in 1947. He was Head of the School of Drawing and Painting at the College from 1960 to 1982. He was elected ARSA in 1952 and RSA in 1962, serving as Secretary of the Academy from 1969 to 1973, when he was elected the sixteenth President of the Academy, retiring in 1983. He was elected ARA in 1973 and RA in 1980.

ANNE REDPATH, RSA, ARA

1895-1965

Born in Galashiels, the daughter of a tweed designer, Anne Redpath overcame initial parental opposition to the study of art and enrolled at Edinburgh College of Art and Moray House College of Education, qualifying as an art teacher in 1917. Awarded a travelling scholarship in 1919, she visited Brussels, Bruges, Paris, Florence and Siena. In 1920 she married an architect with the War Graves Commission in France and settled in northern France before moving to the Riviera. She returned in 1934 to live in Hawick in the Scottish Borders, moving to Edinburgh in 1949. Until then her paintings were mainly still-life and landscapes, but following subsequent visits to Spain, Corsica, the Canary Islands, Portugal and Italy, her subjects included hill-top villages in Corsica and richly ornate altars in Mediterranean churches. She was elected ARSA and RSA in 1947 and 1952 respectively and ARA in 1960.

JOHN GUTHRIE SPENCE SMITH, RSA

1880-1951

Known to his artist friends as 'Dummy Smith', because he was struck deaf and dumb after contracting scarlet fever in infancy, Spence Smith was born in Perth, where his father was a linen draper. He studied at Edinburgh College of Art and at the RSA Life School. He made visits to France with his mother in 1911 and 1912, but he never travelled abroad again. He painted mainly landscapes and architectural subjects. He was a founder-member of the short-lived Edinburgh Group, exhibiting with them in 1912 and 1913 and again in 1919-21 when the Group was re-formed. He exhibited regularly throughout his career at the Royal Scottish Academy and the Royal Glasgow Institute of the Fine Arts. He was elected ARSA in 1930 and RSA in 1939.

MARGARET THOMAS

Born 1916

Born in London, Margaret Thomas studied at the Slade and the Royal Academy Schools in London from 1936 to 1939. She acquired a studio in Edinburgh in 1956 and lived and worked partly in Edinburgh until recently, exhibiting at the Royal Scottish Academy as well as the Royal Academy in London. She now lives in Norfolk.

LEFT
David Alison

Woman Reading by a
Window (457)

Stanley Cursiter

Reclining Lady in White
(403)

John Guthrie Spence Smith
Ballachulish Quarries
(290)

Sir David Muirhead Bone
*The Fair, Ayr Race
Course (245)*

Henry John Lintott
From My Studio Window (372)

97

George Houston
Landscape (The Bluebell Wood) (365)

James McIntosh Patrick
Glamis Village in April (409)

James McBey

Sir William George Gillies
Near Temple (461)
Watercolour

Anne Redpath
The Pink Table (215)

RIGHT
Sir William MacTaggart

Eric Auld

Benachie from Leochel Cushnie
(475)
Oil Pastel

Ian Houston
Loch Eil near Corpach
(484)

Dorothy Johnstone
Bowl of Fruit (319)

Elizabeth Blackadder
Cat and Flowers (378)
Watercolour

Margaret Thomas
Poppies (453)

FOLLOWING PAGE
John Houston
*Poppies and Roses
(448)*

111

113

LEFT
Joan Eardley
Winter Sea III (67)

Robert Henderson Blyth
The Mill Lade (276)
Watercolour

James Maclaughlan Milne
The Harbour at St. Tropez

Donald McIntyre
Portsoy (near Banff)
(445)

John Gardiner Crawford
Christmas Day (320)
Acrylic

James Fairgrieve
Winter Hay (343)
Acrylic

David Donaldson
Arrangement in White

Bronzes

Artists represented

SALLY ARNUP

Born 1930

Sally Arnup studied at the Royal College of Art in London. A sculptor, she specialises in bronzes of birds and animals. In 1971 she sculpted the silver leopard presented to Her Majesty The Queen by the City of York to mark her visit on the occasion of the City's 1,900 years celebrations.

PHYLLIS BONE, RSA

1894-1972

Born at Hornby in Lancashire, Phyllis Bone went to school in Edinburgh and studied sculpture at Edinburgh College of Art and in Paris. She specialised in sculpting animals. She was elected ARSA in 1939 and RSA in 1944, the first woman to be elected an Academician.

MARY FERN FLEMING

Born 1942

Mary Fleming studied drawing in Paris and Italy in 1958-59 and painting and sculpture with Nigel Harcourt-Lees in 1968-69. She lives on a farm in Oxfordshire.

HELEN ANNE LUBBOCK

Born 1919

Helen Lubbock studied at Duncan of Jordanstone College of Art in Dundee. She is a member of the Society of Portrait Sculptors.

Helen Anne Lubbock
Philip Fleming, Esq.
Bronze

Sally Arnup
Standing Pointer Pup
Bronze

Phyllis Bone
The Cushie Doo
Bronze

Mary Fern Fleming
Group of Stag Ponies
Bronze

Index to Artists

Acknowledgements

Robert Fleming Holdings Limited gratefully acknowledge the assistance of Andrew McIntosh Patrick of The Fine Art Society in London, who read the text and made a number of helpful comments. Flemings are also grateful to William Hardie in Glasgow and William Jackson of The Scottish Gallery in Edinburgh.

Flemings also acknowledge the following sources of information relating to artists:
Billcliffe, The Glasgow Boys, London 1985
Caw, Scottish Painting Past and Present: 1620-1908, Edinburgh 1908
Cursiter, Scottish Art, London 1949
Hardie, Scottish Painting 1837-1939, London 1976
Irwin, Scottish Painters at Home and Abroad 1700-1900, London 1975

Exhibition catalogues published by Aberdeen Art Gallery and Museums; Belgrave Gallery, London; Bourne Fine Art, Edinburgh and London; Dundee Museums and Art Galleries; Edinburgh City Art Centre; The Fine Art Society, Edinburgh, Glasgow and London; Cyril Gerber Fine Art, Glasgow; Glasgow Museums and Art Galleries; Lillie Art Gallery, Milngavie; Mercury Gallery, Edinburgh and London; National Galleries of Scotland, Edinburgh; Perth Museum and Art Gallery; Polak Gallery, London; Scottish Arts Council, Edinburgh; The Scottish Gallery, Edinburgh; Talbot Rice Art Centre, University of Edinburgh; Thackeray Gallery, London.